90 Day Focus Planner
&
Notebook
- Business Edition -

Katie Nicholson

Copyright © 2022 Katie Nicholson
All rights reserved.

Thank you for complying with all relevant copyright laws by not reproducing, scanning, or distributing any part of this work in any form without permission. For all enquiries, please contact support@encouragingminds.com.au.

Encouraging Minds, NSW, Australia
support@encouragingminds.com.au

ISBN 13: 978-0-6455680-0-4

There is no express or implied guarantee regarding your individual results from purchasing, completing activities within this planner, or by using this planner in any way. Results may vary from person to person.

Whilst every effort has been made to provide accurate information at the time of publication, neither the author or publisher assumes any responsibility for errors or changes that occur after publication.

For all enquiries re bulk orders and discounts for bulk orders, please contact support@encouragingminds.com.au

Hello,

I am so glad you are here and ready to work in a more focused way in your business. I know what it's like to be distracted by all the ideas or get caught up in busy-work. Without a clear intention each day you can easily be pulled in this or that direction and not make the most effective use of your time or energy. I am not suggesting you optimise every moment for work. By focusing your attention on the most important task or project for the day you give yourself the gift of time and energy for other important activities like time with friends, enjoying nature or non-work-related creative pursuits.

This planner provides a few prompts at the start to guide you in setting your overall focus for the next 90 days, and then for each month. The bulk of the planner is designed to help you focus in on the number one priority for the day, with space to make notes or journal, sketch or draw thumbnails or mind maps - whatever process works best for you. If you would like a little more context or more detailed instructions there is an online companion page to assist you (find details on the Contents page).

This book contains undated pages so you can start whenever suits you. There is no need to wait until January 1. You can choose to use the 'Priority Task' pages only on days you work on your business or for other days as well.

This planner is flexible enough to support entrepreneurs in various businesses and at different stages of their business journey. It is not intended to guide you through *everything* you might need to know or want to do in your business in the next 90 days. It's key function is to *focus* you. It is designed to help you assess what is working (or not) in your business today and what you most want going forward. You will then use the 'Daily Priority Task' pages to get your attention on key activities - tasks that will help you get from where you are now to where you want to be. My hope is that by focusing on what is most important you are able to do *less* and achieve *more*. Getting clear on your priority tasks will help you create a way of working that is more easeful, purposeful and effective, giving you the freedom you really want.

I hope you find this planner and notebook to be a simple and effective tool for your business life. I would love your feedback regarding what works really well for you and what you would like to see added or changed.

Wishing you every success,

Katie

© Katie Nicholson 2022

> Focus on what is important and trust the process.

© Katie Nicholson 2022

Contents

Business Mission, Vision + Values	6
Entrepreneur Business Wheel	8
Entrepreneur Business Wheel Notes	9
90 Day Focus Planning	15
Daily Priority Task and Dot Note Pages	19
Final Reflections	200
Shopping List	202
What's Next?	203

Icon Key

When you see a numbered yellow box like this one: *1* it means you will find bonus resources online that are designed to help you make the best use of the exercise or section.

Bonus Online Resources

katienicholson.co/focus-planner-business

Visit katienicholson.co/focus-planner-business-subscribe and enter your email to get the password for access.

© Katie Nicholson 2022

Business Mission, Vision + Values

Your business has a purpose and you have a vision for what you want for and from your business in the months and years ahead. Record your mission, vision and values for easy reference. This not only keeps your 'why' in focus, it simplifies the goal-setting process. Any time or energy you expend, or any task or project you work on should clearly connect to the reason your business exists and the overall vision or dreams you have for your business in the future. At any time you should be able to stop and satisfactorily answer, "Why am I doing this?"

If you have already defined your mission, vision and values, completing this section will be quick and easy. If you are newer to business you may still be defining these and I have included a few simple questions to help. Make sure your statements are simple, clear and meaningful to you. Completing this section each quarter will give you an interesting insight into what has remained consistent and stable over time, as well as what has shifted and evolved.

What are the core values of your business? These are the values, principles or beliefs that inform and support your mission and vision. If you have many, try to narrow your list to three or to a short phrase incorporating two or three core values.

 Your business values are unique to you. If you would like some examples or inspiration, see this list of values.

My top three Business Values:

In simple terms, your mission is what your business is doing right now and why it is doing it. Consider these questions as you define or describe your mission: Who does your business serve? What do you do or offer your clients or customers? What makes your business unique, different or special?

My Business Mission:

Your business vision is about the ideal future of your business - what it will be and the impact it will ultimately achieve in line with its purpose. What do you want your business to be and do in 1, 3 or 5 years? How will you know your business is successful? How do you want it to grow and when?

My Business Vision:

Now let's look at how satisfied you are with each of the various areas of your business. The *Entrepreneur Business Wheel* on the following page is a tool to help you do that.

 Visit katienicholson.co/focus-planner-business for a larger version and to print more copies.

© Katie Nicholson 2022

Entrepreneur Business Wheel

Score or rate each segment from 1 to 10 for how satisfied you are with this area of your business.

If any area is not relevant for your business rename the wedge with something more useful. For instance "Colleagues + Team" may become "Audience", or "Sales + Marketing" may be divided into two wedges.

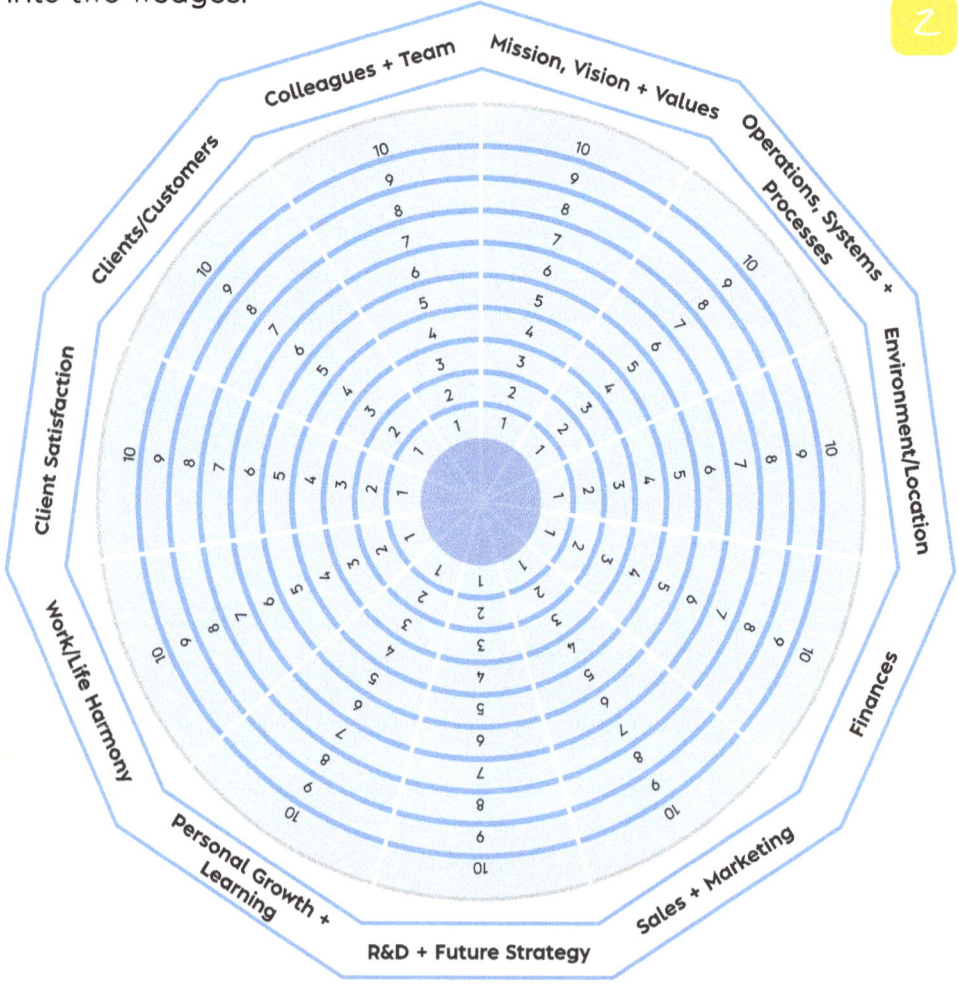

Entrepreneur Business Wheel Notes

The wheel you just completed is a simple yet effective tool. It is most useful when we reflect on our scores and use what we learn to inform our actions. You may have a reasonably even wheel or your scores could vary greatly. Keep your finished wheel and complete this exercise regularly. Notice changes and improvements as you set and achieve goals relating to certain business areas.

To benefit further from using the wheel I have included a half-page section for each area where you can note down whatever seems most important to you. It may be the big challenges you are facing in this area or it could be all your ideas for growth or improvement.

Mission, Vision + Values

Business Wheel Score: /10

First I would like to focus on:

Operations, Systems + Processes

Business Wheel Score: /10

First I would like to focus on:

Environment/Location

Business Wheel Score: /10

First I would like to focus on:

Finances

Business Wheel Score: /10

First I would like to focus on:

Sales + Marketing

Business Wheel Score: /10

First I would like to focus on:

R&D + Future Strategy

Business Wheel Score: /10

First I would like to focus on:

Personal Growth + Learning

Business Wheel Score: /10

First I would like to focus on:

© Katie Nicholson 2022

Work/Life Harmony

Business Wheel Score: /10

First I would like to focus on:

Client Satisfaction

Business Wheel Score: /10

First I would like to focus on:

Clients/Customers

Business Wheel Score: /10

First I would like to focus on:

Colleagues + Team

Business Wheel Score: /10

First I would like to focus on:

90 Day Focus Planning

Now that you have taken some time to review each area of your business you will likely have some new awareness and insights. Take your learnings from the previous section along with your mission, vision and values and decide what you *really* want to put your time and effort towards in the coming months.

Let's focus in on the next 90 days. The next few pages will step you through a few guiding questions.

If you are finding it difficult to prioritise or narrow down your focus, go back to the section that asked for your Business Vision and top three Business Values and read through what you wrote. Look over the business areas in the previous pages and see what you noted down in the small 'focus' boxes. Finally, settle on the one most powerful thing you can do now to move your business forward.

Remember your timeframe is 90 days. Select a project or goal that may feel like a stretch (you might not know how you are going to achieve it yet!), but is possible or realistic to accomplish in 90 days.

What would you most like to achieve or transform in your business in the next 90 days?

Why is this important to you right now?

What top three strengths will be most helpful to you as you work to achieve this goal?

What external support and resources will be most helpful to you as you work to achieve this goal?

What will be your greatest *external* challenge, barrier or distraction to achieving this goal?

What will be your greatest *internal* challenge, barrier or distraction to achieving this goal?

What have you tried in the past to deal with these or similar challenges? How well did that work?

What will you do now to help you to meet this challenge, barrier or distraction successfully?

Congratulations! You are on your way to doing what matters this quarter. Now you need to break it down a little further. Decide on what you will focus on for *each month* this quarter. What is the most important thing you can do or achieve this month to move you closer to your 90 day goal? Ask yourself the same question for the remaining two months. Revisit these goals at the start of each month to make sure they are still the best focus for that month.

What would you most like to achieve in your business in the month of _____ ? Why is it important right now, and how does it connect with your 90 day goal or focus?

What would you most like to achieve in your business in the month of _____ ? Why is it important right now, and how does it connect with your 90 day goal or focus?

What would you most like to achieve in your business in the month of _____ ? Why is it important right now, and how does it connect with your 90 day goal or focus?

What is your very next step?

Daily Priority Task and Dot Note Pages

The Daily Priority Task page is the key feature of this planner. You have set yourself meaningful goals because you are clear on your mission, vision and values. Now you can ensure that the tasks you do each day are clearly connected to and support those goals. The aim of this simply designed page is for you to select the single most important task or project for that day. The task that, if you accomplish it, will move your business forward in the best possible way. Alternatively, you may need to prioritise a task that if *not* completed could greatly impact your business in a negative way.

After settling on your priority task for the day you can list another two to three tasks that are of secondary importance. Notice that I said "secondary importance". These are not filler tasks or time-wasting busywork. Always focus on what is most important first and then move down the ladder of importance.

The prompts at the bottom of the page are designed for a couple minutes of reflection at the end of the day. In a few minutes you will gain key insights, build a grateful perspective and remember to take the time to look after yourself with a renewal activity. There is also space to note which business value will most influence your work for the day. A simple habit tracking section is helpful for when you are working on establishing a new habit.

The dot pages give you both structure and flexibility to use in a way that fits your needs and process. If you want to sketch a mind map or thumbnails for a project, you can do it here. You can use the dot page to write down ideas as they come to you so you can quickly refocus on the task at hand. You may want to use it to list out the steps for a task or add other details. Do whatever helps you best to focus and take strategic action.

 For tips on using each section of the Daily Priority Task page, go to section 5 at katienicholson.co/focus-planner-business.

DAY: DATE:

Today's Priority Task #1

☐ _____

#2 ☐ _____

#3 ☐ _____

Connection

Today I will reach out to...

AM	
PM	

Resources

Today I will access...

Today I am *grateful* for

Today's value focus is

Today's *renewal* activity is

Habit Tracker

Today I will track...

Today's goal is:

○ ○ ○ ○ ○ ○
○ ○ ○ ○ ○ ○

Today's key *insight* is

© Katie Nicholson 2022

DAY: DATE:

Today's Priority Task #1

☐ _____

#2 ☐ _____

#3 ☐ _____

Connection
Today I will reach out to...

AM	
PM	

Resources
Today I will access...

Today I am *grateful* for

Today's *value* focus is

Today's *renewal* activity is

Today's key *insight* is

Habit Tracker
Today I will track...

Today's goal is:
○ ○ ○ ○ ○ ○
○ ○ ○ ○ ○ ○

© Katie Nicholson 2022

DAY: DATE:

Today's Priority Task #1

☐ _____

#2 ☐ _____

#3 ☐ _____

Connection

Today I will reach out to...

AM	
PM	

Resources

Today I will access...

Today I am *grateful* for

Today's value focus is

Today's *renewal* activity is

Habit Tracker

Today I will track...

Today's key *insight* is

Today's goal is:

○ ○ ○ ○ ○ ○
○ ○ ○ ○ ○ ○

© Katie Nicholson 2022

DAY: DATE:

Today's Priority Task #1
☐ _____

#2 ☐ _____

#3 ☐ _____

Connection
Today I will reach out to...

AM	
PM	

Resources
Today I will access...

Today I am *grateful* for

Today's value focus is

Today's *renewal* activity is

Habit Tracker
Today I will track...

Today's goal is:

○ ○ ○ ○ ○ ○
○ ○ ○ ○ ○ ○

Today's key *insight* is

© Katie Nicholson 2022

DAY: DATE:

Today's Priority Task #1

☐ _____

#2 ☐ _____

#3 ☐ _____

Connection

Today I will reach out to...

AM	
PM	

Resources

Today I will access...

Today I am *grateful* for

Today's value focus is

Today's *renewal* activity is

Habit Tracker

Today I will track...

Today's key *insight* is

Today's goal is:

○ ○ ○ ○ ○ ○ ○
○ ○ ○ ○ ○ ○ ○

DAY: DATE:

Today's Priority Task #1

☐ _____

#2 ☐ _____

#3 ☐ _____

AM	
PM	

Today I am *grateful* for

Today's *renewal* activity is

Today's key *insight* is

Connection
Today I will reach out to...

Resources
Today I will access...

Today's *value focus* is

Habit Tracker
Today I will track...

Today's goal is:

○ ○ ○ ○ ○ ○
○ ○ ○ ○ ○ ○

© Katie Nicholson 2022

DAY: DATE:

Today's Priority Task #1
☐ _____

#2 ☐ _____

#3 ☐ _____

Connection
Today I will reach out to...

AM	
PM	

Resources
Today I will access...

Today I am *grateful* for

Today's value focus is

Today's *renewal* activity is

Habit Tracker
Today I will track...

Today's goal is:
○ ○ ○ ○ ○ ○
○ ○ ○ ○ ○ ○

Today's key *insight* is

© Katie Nicholson 2022

DAY: DATE:

Today's Priority Task #1

☐ _____

#2 ☐ _____

#3 ☐ _____

Connection
Today I will reach out to...

AM	
PM	

Resources
Today I will access...

Today I am *grateful* for

Today's *value* focus is

Today's *renewal* activity is

Habit Tracker
Today I will track...

Today's goal is:
○ ○ ○ ○ ○ ○
○ ○ ○ ○ ○ ○

Today's key *insight* is

© Katie Nicholson 2022

DAY: DATE:

Today's Priority Task #1

☐ _____

#2 ☐ _____

#3 ☐ _____

Connection
Today I will reach out to...

AM	
PM	

Resources
Today I will access...

Today I am *grateful* for

Today's *value* focus is

Today's *renewal* activity is

Today's key *insight* is

Habit Tracker
Today I will track...

Today's goal is:
○ ○ ○ ○ ○
○ ○ ○ ○ ○

DAY: DATE:

Today's Priority Task #1

☐ _____

#2 ☐ _____

#3 ☐ _____

Connection

Today I will reach out to...

AM	
PM	

Resources

Today I will access...

Today I am *grateful* for

Today's value focus is

Today's *renewal* activity is

Habit Tracker

Today I will track...

Today's goal is:

○ ○ ○ ○ ○ ○
○ ○ ○ ○ ○ ○

Today's key *insight* is

© Katie Nicholson 2022

© Katie Nicholson 2022

DAY: DATE:

Today's Priority Task #1

☐ _____

#2 ☐ _____

#3 ☐ _____

Connection

Today I will reach out to...

AM	
PM	

Resources

Today I will access...

Today I am *grateful* for

Today's value focus is

Today's *renewal* activity is

Habit Tracker

Today I will track...

Today's key *insight* is

Today's goal is:

○ ○ ○ ○ ○
○ ○ ○ ○ ○

© Katie Nicholson 2022

DAY: DATE:

Today's Priority Task #1

☐ _____

#2 ☐ _____

#3 ☐ _____

Connection

Today I will reach out to...

AM	
PM	

Resources

Today I will access...

Today I am *grateful* for

Today's *value* focus is

Today's *renewal* activity is

Habit Tracker

Today I will track...

Today's goal is:

○ ○ ○ ○ ○
○ ○ ○ ○ ○

Today's key *insight* is

DAY: DATE:

Today's Priority Task #1

☐ _____

#2 ☐ _____

#3 ☐ _____

Connection
Today I will reach out to...

AM	
PM	

Resources
Today I will access...

Today I am *grateful* for

Today's *value* focus is

Today's *renewal* activity is

Habit Tracker
Today I will track...

Today's key *insight* is

Today's goal is:
○ ○ ○ ○ ○ ○
○ ○ ○ ○ ○ ○

© Katie Nicholson 2022

DAY: DATE:

Today's Priority Task #1

☐ _____

#2 ☐ _____

#3 ☐ _____

Connection

Today I will reach out to...

AM	
PM	

Resources

Today I will access...

Today I am *grateful* for

Today's *value* focus is

Today's *renewal* activity is

Habit Tracker

Today I will track...

Today's goal is:

○ ○ ○ ○ ○ ○
○ ○ ○ ○ ○ ○

Today's key *insight* is

DAY: DATE:

Today's Priority Task #1
☐ _____

#2 ☐ _____

#3 ☐ _____

AM	
PM	

Connection
Today I will reach out to...

Resources
Today I will access...

Today I am *grateful* for

Today's *value* focus is

Today's *renewal* activity is

Habit Tracker
Today I will track...

Today's goal is:
○ ○ ○ ○ ○
○ ○ ○ ○ ○

Today's key *insight* is

DAY: DATE:

Today's Priority Task #1

☐ _____

#2 ☐ _____

#3 ☐ _____

Connection

Today I will reach out to...

AM	
PM	

Resources

Today I will access...

Today I am *grateful* for

Today's value focus is

Today's *renewal* activity is

Habit Tracker

Today I will track...

Today's key *insight* is

Today's goal is:

○ ○ ○ ○ ○
○ ○ ○ ○ ○

© Katie Nicholson 2022

DAY: DATE:

Today's Priority Task #1
☐ _____

#2 ☐ _____

#3 ☐ _____

Connection

Today I will reach out to...

AM	
PM	

Resources

Today I will access...

Today I am *grateful* for

Today's *value* focus is

Today's *renewal* activity is

Today's key *insight* is

Habit Tracker

Today I will track...

Today's goal is:

○ ○ ○ ○ ○
○ ○ ○ ○ ○

© Katie Nicholson 2022

DAY: DATE:

Today's Priority Task #1

☐ _____

#2 ☐ _____

#3 ☐ _____

Connection
Today I will reach out to...

AM	
PM	

Resources
Today I will access...

Today I am *grateful* for

Today's *value* focus is

Today's *renewal* activity is

Today's key *insight* is

Habit Tracker
Today I will track...

Today's goal is:

○ ○ ○ ○ ○ ○
○ ○ ○ ○ ○ ○

DAY: DATE:

Today's Priority Task #1
☐ _____

#2 ☐ _____

#3 ☐ _____

Connection
Today I will reach out to...

AM	
PM	

Resources
Today I will access...

Today I am *grateful* for

Today's *value* focus is

Today's *renewal* activity is

Habit Tracker
Today I will track...

Today's goal is:
○ ○ ○ ○ ○ ○
○ ○ ○ ○ ○ ○

Today's key *insight* is

DAY: DATE:

Today's Priority Task #1

☐ _____

#2 ☐ _____

#3 ☐ _____

Connection

Today I will reach out to...

AM	
PM	

Resources

Today I will access...

Today I am *grateful* for

Today's *value* focus is

Today's *renewal* activity is

Today's key *insight* is

Habit Tracker

Today I will track...

Today's goal is:

○ ○ ○ ○ ○ ○
○ ○ ○ ○ ○ ○

© Katie Nicholson 2022

DAY: DATE:

Today's Priority Task #1

☐ _____

#2 ☐ _____

#3 ☐ _____

Connection

Today I will reach out to...

AM	
PM	

Resources

Today I will access...

Today I am *grateful* for

Today's *value* focus is

Today's *renewal* activity is

Habit Tracker

Today I will track...

Today's goal is:

○ ○ ○ ○ ○ ○
○ ○ ○ ○ ○ ○

Today's key *insight* is

© Katie Nicholson 2022   61

DAY: DATE:

Today's Priority Task #1

☐ _____

#2 ☐ _____

#3 ☐ _____

Connection

Today I will reach out to...

AM	
PM	

Resources

Today I will access...

Today I am *grateful* for

Today's value focus is

Today's *renewal* activity is

Habit Tracker

Today I will track...

Today's goal is:

○ ○ ○ ○ ○
○ ○ ○ ○ ○

Today's key *insight* is

DAY: DATE:

Today's Priority Task #1
- [ ] _____

   #2 [ ] _____

   #3 [ ] _____

Connection
Today I will reach out to...

AM	
PM	

Resources
Today I will access...

Today I am *grateful* for

Today's *value focus* is

Today's *renewal* activity is

Habit Tracker
Today I will track...

Today's goal is:
○ ○ ○ ○ ○
○ ○ ○ ○ ○

Today's key *insight* is

© Katie Nicholson 2022

DAY: DATE:

Today's Priority Task #1

☐ _____

#2 ☐ _____

#3 ☐ _____

Connection

Today I will reach out to...

AM	
PM	

Resources

Today I will access...

Today I am *grateful* for

Today's *value* focus is

Today's *renewal* activity is

Today's key *insight* is

Habit Tracker

Today I will track...

Today's goal is:

○ ○ ○ ○ ○
○ ○ ○ ○ ○

© Katie Nicholson 2022

DAY: DATE:

Today's Priority Task #1
☐ _____

#2 ☐ _____

#3 ☐ _____

Connection
Today I will reach out to...

AM	
PM	

Resources
Today I will access...

Today I am *grateful* for

Today's value focus is

Today's *renewal* activity is

Habit Tracker
Today I will track...

Today's goal is:
○ ○ ○ ○ ○
○ ○ ○ ○ ○

Today's key *insight* is

DAY: DATE:

Today's Priority Task #1

☐ _____

#2 ☐ _____

#3 ☐ _____

Connection

Today I will reach out to...

AM	
PM	

Resources

Today I will access...

Today I am *grateful* for

Today's value focus is

Today's *renewal* activity is

Habit Tracker

Today I will track...

Today's key *insight* is

Today's goal is:

○ ○ ○ ○ ○
○ ○ ○ ○ ○

© Katie Nicholson 2022

DAY: DATE:

Today's Priority Task #1
☐ _____

#2 ☐ _____

#3 ☐ _____

Connection
Today I will reach out to...

AM	
PM	

Resources
Today I will access...

Today I am *grateful* for

Today's *value* focus is

Today's *renewal* activity is

Today's key *insight* is

Habit Tracker
Today I will track...

Today's goal is:
○ ○ ○ ○ ○ ○
○ ○ ○ ○ ○ ○

© Katie Nicholson 2022

DAY: DATE:

Today's Priority Task #1
☐ _____

#2 ☐ _____

#3 ☐ _____

Connection
Today I will reach out to...

AM	
PM	

Resources
Today I will access...

Today I am *grateful* for

Today's *value* focus is

Today's *renewal* activity is

Habit Tracker
Today I will track...

Today's key *insight* is

Today's goal is:
○ ○ ○ ○ ○
○ ○ ○ ○ ○

© Katie Nicholson 2022

DAY: DATE:

Today's Priority Task #1
☐ _____

#2 ☐ _____

#3 ☐ _____

Connection
Today I will reach out to...

AM	
PM	

Resources
Today I will access...

Today I am *grateful* for

Today's *value* focus is

Today's *renewal* activity is

Habit Tracker
Today I will track...

Today's goal is:
○ ○ ○ ○ ○
○ ○ ○ ○ ○

Today's key *insight* is

Are you enjoying using this 90 Day Focus Planner?
Are you achieving more of what matters with less overwhelm and time-wasting?
Remember to visit katienicholson.co for more resources to help you design a business life that works for you.

© Katie Nicholson 2022

DAY: DATE:

Today's Priority Task #1

☐ _____

#2 ☐ _____

#3 ☐ _____

Connection
Today I will reach out to...

AM	
PM	

Resources
Today I will access...

Today I am *grateful* for

Today's *value* focus is

Today's *renewal* activity is

Habit Tracker
Today I will track...

Today's goal is:

○ ○ ○ ○ ○ ○
○ ○ ○ ○ ○ ○

Today's key *insight* is

© Katie Nicholson 2022

DAY: DATE:

Today's Priority Task #1
☐ _____

#2 ☐ _____

#3 ☐ _____

Connection
Today I will reach out to...

AM	
PM	

Resources
Today I will access...

Today I am *grateful* for

Today's *value* focus is

Today's *renewal* activity is

Habit Tracker
Today I will track...

Today's goal is:
○ ○ ○ ○ ○
○ ○ ○ ○ ○

Today's key *insight* is

© Katie Nicholson 2022

DAY: DATE:

Today's Priority Task #1
- ☐ _____
  - #2 ☐ _____
  - #3 ☐ _____

Connection
Today I will reach out to...

AM	
PM	

Resources
Today I will access...

Today I am *grateful* for

Today's value focus is

Today's *renewal* activity is

Habit Tracker
Today I will track...

Today's key *insight* is

Today's goal is:
○ ○ ○ ○ ○ ○
○ ○ ○ ○ ○ ○

DAY: DATE:

Today's Priority Task #1
☐ _____

#2 ☐ _____

#3 ☐ _____

Connection
Today I will reach out to...

AM	
PM	

Resources
Today I will access...

Today I am *grateful* for

Today's *value* focus is

Today's *renewal* activity is

Habit Tracker
Today I will track...

Today's goal is:
○ ○ ○ ○ ○
○ ○ ○ ○ ○

Today's key *insight* is

DAY: DATE:

Today's Priority Task #1

☐ _____

    #2 ☐ _____

    #3 ☐ _____

Connection

Today I will reach out to...

AM	
PM	

Resources

Today I will access...

Today I am *grateful* for

Today's value focus is

Today's *renewal* activity is

Habit Tracker

Today I will track...

Today's key *insight* is

Today's goal is:

○ ○ ○ ○ ○
○ ○ ○ ○ ○

© Katie Nicholson 2022

DAY: DATE:

Today's Priority Task #1
- [ ] _____

#2 [ ] _____

#3 [ ] _____

Connection

Today I will reach out to...

AM	
PM	

Resources

Today I will access...

Today I am *grateful* for

Today's *value* focus is

Today's *renewal* activity is

Habit Tracker

Today I will track...

Today's goal is:

○ ○ ○ ○ ○ ○
○ ○ ○ ○ ○ ○

Today's key *insight* is

© Katie Nicholson 2022

DAY: DATE:

Today's Priority Task #1

☐ _____

#2 ☐ _____

#3 ☐ _____

Connection
Today I will reach out to...

AM	
PM	

Resources
Today I will access...

Today I am *grateful* for

Today's *value* focus is

Today's *renewal* activity is

Habit Tracker
Today I will track...

Today's goal is:

○ ○ ○ ○ ○ ○
○ ○ ○ ○ ○ ○

Today's key *insight* is

DAY: DATE:

Today's Priority Task #1
☐ _____

#2 ☐ _____

#3 ☐ _____

Connection
Today I will reach out to…

AM	
PM	

Resources
Today I will access…

Today I am *grateful* for

Today's *value* focus is

Today's *renewal* activity is

Habit Tracker
Today I will track…

Today's key *insight* is

Today's goal is:
○ ○ ○ ○ ○
○ ○ ○ ○ ○

© Katie Nicholson 2022

DAY: DATE:

Today's Priority Task #1
☐ _____

#2 ☐ _____

#3 ☐ _____

Connection

Today I will reach out to...

AM	
PM	

Resources

Today I will access...

Today I am *grateful* for

Today's value focus is

Today's *renewal* activity is

Habit Tracker

Today I will track...

Today's key *insight* is

Today's goal is:

○ ○ ○ ○ ○ ○
○ ○ ○ ○ ○ ○

DAY: DATE:

Today's Priority Task #1
☐ _____

#2 ☐ _____

#3 ☐ _____

Connection
Today I will reach out to...

AM	
PM	

Resources
Today I will access...

Today I am *grateful* for

Today's *value* focus is

Today's *renewal* activity is

Today's key *insight* is

Habit Tracker
Today I will track...

Today's goal is:
○ ○ ○ ○ ○ ○
○ ○ ○ ○ ○ ○

DAY: DATE:

Today's Priority Task #1

☐ _____

#2 ☐ _____

#3 ☐ _____

Connection

Today I will reach out to...

AM	
PM	

Resources

Today I will access...

Today I am *grateful* for

Today's *value* focus is

Today's *renewal* activity is

Today's key *insight* is

Habit Tracker

Today I will track...

Today's goal is:

○ ○ ○ ○ ○
○ ○ ○ ○ ○

© Katie Nicholson 2022

DAY:　　　　　　　DATE:

Today's Priority Task #1

☐ _____

#2 ☐ _____

#3 ☐ _____

Connection

Today I will reach out to...

AM	
PM	

Resources

Today I will access...

Today I am *grateful* for

Today's *value* focus is

Today's *renewal* activity is

Habit Tracker

Today I will track...

Today's goal is:

○ ○ ○ ○ ○ ○
○ ○ ○ ○ ○ ○

Today's key *insight* is

© Katie Nicholson 2022

DAY: DATE:

Today's Priority Task #1

☐ _____

#2 ☐ _____

#3 ☐ _____

Connection

Today I will reach out to...

AM	
PM	

Resources

Today I will access...

Today I am *grateful* for

Today's *value* focus is

Today's *renewal* activity is

Today's key *insight* is

Habit Tracker

Today I will track...

Today's goal is:

○ ○ ○ ○ ○ ○
○ ○ ○ ○ ○ ○

DAY: DATE:

Today's Priority Task #1

☐ _____

#2 ☐ _____

#3 ☐ _____

Connection

Today I will reach out to...

AM	
PM	

Resources

Today I will access...

Today I am *grateful* for

Today's value focus is

Today's *renewal* activity is

Habit Tracker

Today I will track...

Today's key *insight* is

Today's goal is:

○ ○ ○ ○ ○
○ ○ ○ ○ ○

DAY: DATE:

Today's Priority Task #1
☐ _____

#2 ☐ _____

#3 ☐ _____

Connection
Today I will reach out to...

AM	
PM	

Resources
Today I will access...

Today I am *grateful* for

Today's *value* focus is

Today's *renewal* activity is

Habit Tracker
Today I will track...

Today's key *insight* is

Today's goal is:
○ ○ ○ ○ ○ ○ ○
○ ○ ○ ○ ○ ○ ○

DAY: DATE:

Today's Priority Task #1

☐ _____

#2 ☐ _____

#3 ☐ _____

Connection

Today I will reach out to...

AM	
PM	

Resources

Today I will access...

Today I am *grateful* for

Today's *value* focus is

Today's *renewal* activity is

Habit Tracker

Today I will track...

Today's key *insight* is

Today's goal is:

○ ○ ○ ○ ○ ○
○ ○ ○ ○ ○ ○

DAY: DATE:

Today's Priority Task #1
☐ _____

#2 ☐ _____

#3 ☐ _____

Connection
Today I will reach out to...

AM	
PM	

Resources
Today I will access...

Today I am *grateful* for

Today's *value* focus is

Today's *renewal* activity is

Habit Tracker
Today I will track...

Today's goal is:
○ ○ ○ ○ ○
○ ○ ○ ○ ○

Today's key *insight* is

© Katie Nicholson 2022

DAY: DATE:

Today's Priority Task #1

☐ _____

   #2 ☐ _____

   #3 ☐ _____

Connection

Today I will reach out to...

AM	
PM	

Resources

Today I will access...

Today I am *grateful* for

Today's value focus is

Today's *renewal* activity is

Habit Tracker

Today I will track...

Today's key *insight* is

Today's goal is:

○ ○ ○ ○ ○
○ ○ ○ ○ ○

DAY: DATE:

Today's Priority Task #1
☐ _____

#2 ☐ _____

#3 ☐ _____

Connection

Today I will reach out to...

AM	
PM	

Resources

Today I will access...

Today I am *grateful* for

Today's *value* focus is

Today's *renewal* activity is

Today's key *insight* is

Habit Tracker

Today I will track...

Today's goal is:

○ ○ ○ ○ ○
○ ○ ○ ○ ○

DAY: _____ DATE: _____

Today's Priority Task #1
- ☐ _____

  #2 ☐ _____

  #3 ☐ _____

Connection
Today I will reach out to...

AM	
PM	

Resources
Today I will access...

Today I am *grateful* for

Today's *value* focus is

Today's *renewal* activity is

Today's key *insight* is

Habit Tracker
Today I will track...

Today's goal is:
○ ○ ○ ○ ○
○ ○ ○ ○ ○

DAY: DATE:

Today's Priority Task #1
☐ _____

    #2 ☐ _____

    #3 ☐ _____

Connection

Today I will reach out to...

AM	
PM	

Resources

Today I will access...

Today I am *grateful* for

Today's *value* focus is

Today's *renewal* activity is

Habit Tracker

Today I will track...

Today's goal is:

○ ○ ○ ○ ○
○ ○ ○ ○ ○

Today's key *insight* is

© Katie Nicholson 2022

DAY: DATE:

Today's Priority Task #1

☐ _____

#2 ☐ _____

#3 ☐ _____

Connection

Today I will reach out to...

AM	
PM	

Resources

Today I will access...

Today I am *grateful* for

Today's *value* focus is

Today's *renewal* activity is

Today's key *insight* is

Habit Tracker

Today I will track...

Today's goal is:

○ ○ ○ ○ ○
○ ○ ○ ○ ○

© Katie Nicholson 2022

DAY: DATE:

Today's Priority Task #1

☐ _____

  #2 ☐ _____

  #3 ☐ _____

Connection

Today I will reach out to…

AM	
PM	

Resources

Today I will access…

Today I am *grateful* for

Today's value focus is

Today's *renewal* activity is

Habit Tracker

Today I will track…

Today's key *insight* is

Today's goal is:

○ ○ ○ ○ ○
○ ○ ○ ○ ○

© Katie Nicholson 2022

DAY: DATE:

Today's Priority Task #1

☐ _____

   #2 ☐ _____

   #3 ☐ _____

Connection

Today I will reach out to...

AM	
PM	

Resources

Today I will access...

Today I am *grateful* for

Today's *value* focus is

Today's *renewal* activity is

Habit Tracker

Today I will track...

Today's goal is:

○ ○ ○ ○ ○
○ ○ ○ ○ ○

Today's key *insight* is

© Katie Nicholson 2022

DAY: DATE:

Today's Priority Task #1
- ☐ _____

    #2 ☐ _____

    #3 ☐ _____

Connection
Today I will reach out to...

AM	
PM	

Resources
Today I will access...

Today I am *grateful* for

Today's value focus is

Today's *renewal* activity is

Today's key *insight* is

Habit Tracker
Today I will track...

Today's goal is:
○ ○ ○ ○ ○ ○ ○
○ ○ ○ ○ ○ ○ ○

© Katie Nicholson 2022

DAY: DATE:

Today's Priority Task #1

☐ _____

#2 ☐ _____

#3 ☐ _____

Connection

Today I will reach out to...

AM	
PM	

Resources

Today I will access...

Today I am *grateful* for

Today's *value* focus is

Today's *renewal* activity is

Today's key *insight* is

Habit Tracker

Today I will track...

Today's goal is:

○ ○ ○ ○ ○ ○
○ ○ ○ ○ ○ ○

Are you enjoying using this 90 Day Focus Planner? Are you achieving more of what matters with less overwhelm and time-wasting? Purchase your next 90 Day Focus Planner now and be ready for the next Quarter.

DAY: DATE:

Today's Priority Task #1

☐ _____

     #2 ☐ _____

     #3 ☐ _____

Connection

Today I will reach out to…

AM	
PM	

Resources

Today I will access…

Today I am *grateful* for

Today's *value* focus is

Today's *renewal* activity is

Today's key *insight* is

Habit Tracker

Today I will track…

Today's goal is:

○ ○ ○ ○ ○
○ ○ ○ ○ ○

DAY: DATE:

Today's Priority Task #1
- ☐ _____

    #2 ☐ _____

    #3 ☐ _____

Connection
Today I will reach out to...

AM	
PM	

Resources
Today I will access...

Today I am *grateful* for

Today's *value* focus is

Today's *renewal* activity is

Today's key *insight* is

Habit Tracker
Today I will track...

Today's goal is:
○ ○ ○ ○ ○ ○
○ ○ ○ ○ ○ ○

DAY: DATE:

Today's Priority Task #1
☐ _____

#2 ☐ _____

#3 ☐ _____

Connection
Today I will reach out to...

AM	
PM	

Resources
Today I will access...

Today I am *grateful* for

Today's *value* focus is

Today's *renewal* activity is

Today's key *insight* is

Habit Tracker
Today I will track...

Today's goal is:
○ ○ ○ ○ ○
○ ○ ○ ○ ○

© Katie Nicholson 2022

DAY: DATE:

Today's Priority Task #1
☐ _____

#2 ☐ _____

#3 ☐ _____

Connection
Today I will reach out to...

AM	
PM	

Resources
Today I will access...

Today I am *grateful* for

Today's *value* focus is

Today's *renewal* activity is

Habit Tracker
Today I will track...

Today's goal is:
○ ○ ○ ○ ○
○ ○ ○ ○ ○

Today's key *insight* is

© Katie Nicholson 2022

DAY: DATE:

Today's Priority Task #1
- ☐ _____

    #2 ☐ _____

    #3 ☐ _____

Connection
Today I will reach out to...

AM	
PM	

Resources
Today I will access...

Today I am *grateful* for

Today's value focus is

Today's *renewal* activity is

Habit Tracker
Today I will track...

Today's goal is:

○ ○ ○ ○ ○
○ ○ ○ ○ ○

Today's key *insight* is

DAY: DATE:

Today's Priority Task #1

☐ _____

#2 ☐ _____

#3 ☐ _____

Connection

Today I will reach out to...

AM	
PM	

Resources

Today I will access...

Today I am *grateful* for

Today's *value* focus is

Today's *renewal* activity is

Today's key *insight* is

Habit Tracker

Today I will track...

Today's goal is:

○ ○ ○ ○ ○
○ ○ ○ ○ ○

DAY: DATE:

Today's Priority Task #1

☐ _____

#2 ☐ _____

#3 ☐ _____

Connection
Today I will reach out to...

AM	
PM	

Resources
Today I will access...

Today I am *grateful* for

Today's value focus is

Today's *renewal* activity is

Today's key *insight* is

Habit Tracker
Today I will track...

Today's goal is:
○ ○ ○ ○ ○
○ ○ ○ ○ ○

© Katie Nicholson 2022

DAY: DATE:

Today's Priority Task #1
☐ _____

#2 ☐ _____

#3 ☐ _____

Connection

Today I will reach out to...

AM	
PM	

Resources

Today I will access...

Today I am *grateful* for

Today's *value* focus is

Today's *renewal* activity is

Habit Tracker

Today I will track...

Today's goal is:

○ ○ ○ ○ ○
○ ○ ○ ○ ○

Today's key *insight* is

DAY:　　　　　　DATE:

Today's Priority Task #1
☐ _____

   #2 ☐ _____

   #3 ☐ _____

Connection
Today I will reach out to...

AM	
PM	

Resources
Today I will access...

Today I am *grateful* for

Today's *value* focus is

Today's *renewal* activity is

Habit Tracker
Today I will track...

Today's goal is:
○ ○ ○ ○ ○
○ ○ ○ ○ ○

Today's key *insight* is

© Katie Nicholson 2022

DAY: DATE:

Today's Priority Task #1

☐ _____

    #2 ☐ _____

    #3 ☐ _____

Connection
Today I will reach out to...

AM	
PM	

Resources
Today I will access...

Today I am *grateful* for

Today's *value* focus is

Today's *renewal* activity is

Habit Tracker
Today I will track...

Today's goal is:
○ ○ ○ ○ ○ ○
○ ○ ○ ○ ○ ○

Today's key *insight* is

© Katie Nicholson 2022

© Katie Nicholson 2022

DAY: DATE:

Today's Priority Task #1

☐ _____

#2 ☐ _____

#3 ☐ _____

Connection

Today I will reach out to...

AM	
PM	

Resources

Today I will access...

Today I am *grateful* for

Today's *value* focus is

Today's *renewal* activity is

Today's key *insight* is

Habit Tracker

Today I will track...

Today's goal is:

○ ○ ○ ○ ○
○ ○ ○ ○ ○

DAY: DATE:

Today's Priority Task #1

☐ _____

  #2 ☐ _____

  #3 ☐ _____

Connection

Today I will reach out to...

AM	
PM	

Resources

Today I will access...

Today I am *grateful* for

Today's *value* focus is

Today's *renewal* activity is

Today's key *insight* is

Habit Tracker

Today I will track...

Today's goal is:

○ ○ ○ ○ ○
○ ○ ○ ○ ○

© Katie Nicholson 2022

© Katie Nicholson 2022

DAY: DATE:

Today's Priority Task #1

☐ _____

#2 ☐ _____

#3 ☐ _____

Connection

Today I will reach out to...

AM	
PM	

Resources

Today I will access...

Today I am *grateful* for

Today's value focus is

Today's *renewal* activity is

Habit Tracker

Today I will track...

Today's goal is:

○ ○ ○ ○ ○
○ ○ ○ ○ ○

Today's key *insight* is

DAY: DATE:

Today's Priority Task #1

☐ _____

#2 ☐ _____

#3 ☐ _____

Connection

Today I will reach out to...

AM	
PM	

Resources

Today I will access...

Today I am *grateful* for

Today's *value* focus is

Today's *renewal* activity is

Habit Tracker

Today I will track...

Today's key *insight* is

Today's goal is:

○ ○ ○ ○ ○ ○
○ ○ ○ ○ ○ ○

© Katie Nicholson 2022

DAY: DATE:

Today's Priority Task #1

☐ _____

#2 ☐ _____

#3 ☐ _____

Connection

Today I will reach out to...

AM	
PM	

Resources

Today I will access...

Today I am *grateful* for

Today's *value* focus is

Today's *renewal* activity is

Habit Tracker

Today I will track...

Today's goal is:

○ ○ ○ ○ ○
○ ○ ○ ○ ○

Today's key *insight* is

DAY:　　　　　　　　DATE:

Today's Priority Task #1
- ☐ _____

　#2 ☐ _____

　#3 ☐ _____

Connection
Today I will reach out to...

AM	
PM	

Resources
Today I will access...

Today I am *grateful* for

Today's value focus is

Today's *renewal* activity is

Today's key *insight* is

Habit Tracker
Today I will track...

Today's goal is:
○ ○ ○ ○ ○ ○
○ ○ ○ ○ ○ ○

DAY: DATE:

Today's Priority Task #1

☐ _____

   #2 ☐ _____

   #3 ☐ _____

Connection
Today I will reach out to…

AM	
PM	

Resources
Today I will access…

Today I am *grateful* for

Today's *value* focus is

Today's *renewal* activity is

Today's key *insight* is

Habit Tracker
Today I will track…

Today's goal is:

○ ○ ○ ○ ○
○ ○ ○ ○ ○

DAY: DATE:

Today's Priority Task #1

☐ _____

#2 ☐ _____

#3 ☐ _____

Connection
Today I will reach out to...

AM	
PM	

Resources
Today I will access...

Today I am *grateful* for

Today's *value* focus is

Today's *renewal* activity is

Today's key *insight* is

Habit Tracker
Today I will track...

Today's goal is:
○ ○ ○ ○ ○ ○
○ ○ ○ ○ ○ ○

© Katie Nicholson 2022

DAY: DATE:

Today's Priority Task #1

☐ _____

#2 ☐ _____

#3 ☐ _____

Connection
Today I will reach out to...

AM	
PM	

Resources
Today I will access...

Today I am *grateful* for

Today's *value* focus is

Today's *renewal* activity is

Today's key *insight* is

Habit Tracker
Today I will track...

Today's goal is:
○ ○ ○ ○ ○
○ ○ ○ ○ ○

© Katie Nicholson 2022

DAY: DATE:

Today's Priority Task #1
☐ _____

#2 ☐ _____

#3 ☐ _____

Connection
Today I will reach out to...

AM	
PM	

Resources
Today I will access...

Today I am *grateful* for

Today's *value* focus is

Today's *renewal* activity is

Habit Tracker
Today I will track...

Today's goal is:
○ ○ ○ ○ ○
○ ○ ○ ○ ○

Today's key *insight* is

© Katie Nicholson 2022

DAY: DATE:

Today's Priority Task #1
☐ _____

#2 ☐ _____

#3 ☐ _____

Connection
Today I will reach out to...

AM	
PM	

Resources
Today I will access...

Today I am *grateful* for

Today's *value* focus is

Today's *renewal* activity is

Today's key *insight* is

Habit Tracker
Today I will track...

Today's goal is:
○ ○ ○ ○ ○
○ ○ ○ ○ ○

© Katie Nicholson 2022

DAY:　　　　　　DATE:

Today's Priority Task #1
- ☐ _____

　#2 ☐ _____

　#3 ☐ _____

Connection
Today I will reach out to…

AM	
PM	

Resources
Today I will access…

Today I am *grateful* for

Today's value focus is

Today's *renewal* activity is

Today's key *insight* is

Habit Tracker
Today I will track…

Today's goal is:
○ ○ ○ ○ ○ ○
○ ○ ○ ○ ○ ○

© Katie Nicholson 2022

DAY: DATE:

Today's Priority Task #1

☐ _____

#2 ☐ _____

#3 ☐ _____

AM	
PM	

Connection
Today I will reach out to...

Resources
Today I will access...

Today I am *grateful* for

Today's *value* focus is

Today's *renewal* activity is

Habit Tracker
Today I will track...

Today's goal is:
○ ○ ○ ○ ○
○ ○ ○ ○ ○

Today's key *insight* is

© Katie Nicholson 2022

© Katie Nicholson 2022

DAY: DATE:

Today's Priority Task #1

☐ _____

   #2 ☐ _____

   #3 ☐ _____

Connection

Today I will reach out to…

AM	
PM	

Resources

Today I will access…

Today I am *grateful* for

Today's *value* focus is

Today's *renewal* activity is

Today's key *insight* is

Habit Tracker

Today I will track…

Today's goal is:

○ ○ ○ ○ ○
○ ○ ○ ○ ○

© Katie Nicholson 2022

DAY: DATE:

Today's Priority Task #1

☐ _____

   #2 ☐ _____

   #3 ☐ _____

Connection

Today I will reach out to...

AM	
PM	

Resources

Today I will access...

Today I am *grateful* for

Today's *value* focus is

Today's *renewal* activity is

Habit Tracker

Today I will track...

Today's goal is:

○ ○ ○ ○ ○ ○ ○
○ ○ ○ ○ ○ ○ ○

Today's key *insight* is

DAY: DATE:

Today's Priority Task #1
- ☐ _____

　#2 ☐ _____

　#3 ☐ _____

Connection

Today I will reach out to...

AM	
PM	

Resources

Today I will access...

Today I am *grateful* for

Today's value focus is

Today's *renewal* activity is

Habit Tracker

Today I will track...

Today's key *insight* is

Today's goal is:

○ ○ ○ ○ ○
○ ○ ○ ○ ○

© Katie Nicholson 2022

DAY: DATE:

Today's Priority Task #1

☐ _____

   #2 ☐ _____

   #3 ☐ _____

Connection

Today I will reach out to...

AM	
PM	

Resources

Today I will access...

Today I am *grateful* for

Today's *value* focus is

Today's *renewal* activity is

Today's key *insight* is

Habit Tracker

Today I will track...

Today's goal is:

○ ○ ○ ○ ○
○ ○ ○ ○ ○

DAY: DATE:

Today's Priority Task #1
☐ _____

#2 ☐ _____

#3 ☐ _____

Connection
Today I will reach out to…

AM	
PM	

Resources
Today I will access…

Today I am *grateful* for

Today's *value* focus is

Today's *renewal* activity is

Today's key *insight* is

Habit Tracker
Today I will track…

Today's goal is:
○ ○ ○ ○ ○
○ ○ ○ ○ ○

© Katie Nicholson 2022

DAY: DATE:

Today's Priority Task #1

☐ _____

#2 ☐ _____

#3 ☐ _____

Connection

Today I will reach out to...

AM	
PM	

Resources

Today I will access...

Today I am *grateful* for

Today's value focus is

Today's *renewal* activity is

Today's key *insight* is

Habit Tracker

Today I will track...

Today's goal is:

○ ○ ○ ○ ○ ○
○ ○ ○ ○ ○ ○

© Katie Nicholson 2022

DAY: DATE:

Today's Priority Task #1

☐ _____

#2 ☐ _____

#3 ☐ _____

Connection
Today I will reach out to...

AM	
PM	

Resources
Today I will access...

Today I am *grateful* for

Today's *value* focus is

Today's *renewal* activity is

Today's key *insight* is

Habit Tracker
Today I will track...

Today's goal is:
○ ○ ○ ○ ○ ○
○ ○ ○ ○ ○ ○

© Katie Nicholson 2022

DAY: DATE:

Today's Priority Task #1

- ☐ _____

    #2 ☐ _____

    #3 ☐ _____

Connection

Today I will reach out to...

AM	
PM	

Resources

Today I will access...

Today I am *grateful* for

Today's value focus is

Today's *renewal* activity is

Today's key *insight* is

Habit Tracker

Today I will track...

Today's goal is:

○ ○ ○ ○ ○ ○
○ ○ ○ ○ ○ ○

DAY: DATE:

Today's Priority Task #1

☐ _____

　#2 ☐ _____

　#3 ☐ _____

Connection
Today I will reach out to...

AM	
PM	

Resources
Today I will access...

Today I am *grateful* for

Today's *value* focus is

Today's *renewal* activity is

Today's key *insight* is

Habit Tracker
Today I will track...

Today's goal is:
○ ○ ○ ○ ○ ○
○ ○ ○ ○ ○ ○

© Katie Nicholson 2022

DAY: DATE:

Today's Priority Task #1

☐ _____

#2 ☐ _____

#3 ☐ _____

Connection

Today I will reach out to...

AM	
PM	

Resources

Today I will access...

Today I am *grateful* for

Today's *value* focus is

Today's *renewal* activity is

Today's key *insight* is

Habit Tracker

Today I will track...

Today's goal is:

○ ○ ○ ○ ○
○ ○ ○ ○ ○

DAY: DATE:

Today's Priority Task #1
☐ _____

#2 ☐ _____

#3 ☐ _____

Connection
Today I will reach out to...

AM	
PM	

Resources
Today I will access...

Today I am *grateful* for

Today's *value* focus is

Today's *renewal* activity is

Today's key *insight* is

Habit Tracker
Today I will track...

Today's goal is:
○ ○ ○ ○ ○ ○ ○
○ ○ ○ ○ ○ ○ ○

© Katie Nicholson 2022

DAY: DATE:

Today's Priority Task #1

☐ _____

#2 ☐ _____

#3 ☐ _____

Connection

Today I will reach out to...

AM	
PM	

Resources

Today I will access...

Today I am *grateful* for

Today's *value* focus is

Today's *renewal* activity is

Today's key *insight* is

Habit Tracker

Today I will track...

Today's goal is:

○ ○ ○ ○ ○ ○ ○
○ ○ ○ ○ ○ ○ ○

Final Reflections

Congratulations! You did it. You set a focus, goals and intentions over the past 90 days and took focused action. Now it is time to reflect on your experience, your wins and your failures.

As you reflect on your results and any shifts to how you worked consider what was effective. Note also what was easy or fun. Look too at what didn't work so well or what was especially challenging. Were you able to overcome obstacles? Was it worth it? You get to decide. Remember to experiment, reflect on results and pivot as necessary.

Write your responses to the reflective questions. Remember to celebrate before you move into planning the next 90 days.

Looking back at your 90 day focus, how well did you achieve what you set out to achieve and what were the specific results?

Looking back at the past 90 days in business, what are you most proud of?

What was the greatest challenge or barrier to achieving your goal and how did you overcome or address it?

What would you like to do differently next time to address this challenge? What support or resources would you need?

What was a failure you experienced? What did you learn from it and what would you like to do differently next time?

What 'bonus' win or benefit did you experience that was unplanned or unexpected? What did you learn?

Shopping List

What's Next?

Thanks so much for investing in yourself and your business. I know how easy it can be to get caught up in busy-work or to get excited (ie. distracted) by *all* the ideas. Setting the right focus and realigning your work priorities will bring quicker results and a calmer way of being.

If you found this planner helpful I would love to support you in other ways. To discover options for learning, support or working with me start by visiting katienicholson.co.

If you are unable to find what you are looking for please reach out using the contact form or email support@katienicholson.co.

If you are not already part of my email letters community, subscribe at katienicholson.co/subscribe. This is the best place to be kept up to date with learning, inspiration and the latest offerings and resources.

And finally, remember to order your next *90 Day Focus Planner & Notebook - Business Edition* or ask your local bookseller to order one in for you. If you know someone who might benefit from a little more focus in their work grab them a copy too.

Wishing you every success.

Katie

Creator: Katie Nicholson is an Associate Certified Coach (ACC) credentialed with the International Coaching Federation (ICF) and is currently based in Sydney, Australia. Her coaching career officially began with foundational leadership and coaching training in California in 2018.

Katie combines her strengths, continued learning and her professional development with the experience of working for herself in various businesses to support her clients in their individual business journeys. She enjoys working with busy and often overwhelmed female business owners around the world to reset their thinking, get clear on what they really want and draw on their many resources to get results. Through creating a thinking space, shifting unhelpful mindsets and helping her clients understand and use their energy strategically, Katie supports her clients to make the impact they want to make and see the results they have been looking for without sacrificing their wellbeing.

You can reach Katie by email at support@katienicholson.co or keep up to date through her newsletter which you can subscribe to at katienicholson.co/subscribe.

Kind Words from Coaching Clients:

"In our work together [Katie] has helped me understand and commit to doing what I need to do to achieve my personal and business goals. She's a gentle but subtly firm coach." - Jill B.

"I have accomplished more in my business in the last six months than in the previous six years. Sincerely thank you Katie, I look forward to working with you again." - Vanessa P.